December

Blessed are you among women

Prepare the way for the Lord

Men will see the son of man coming on a cloud

Justice shall flourish in his time, and fullness of peace for ever.

Illustrations for Advent and Christmas liturgies - useful for making your own Christmas cards.

TODAY YOU WILL KNOW THAT THE LORD IS COMING TO SAVE US AND IN THE MORNING YOU WILL SEE HIS GLORY.

December 4

They found Mary and Joseph, and the baby lying in a manger

May the peace of Christ rule in your hearts and the fullness of his message live within you.

All who heard him were amazed at his intelligence and his answers.

Advent and Christmas themes of the Community in Church

Offertory

The Advent wreath

Choir practice – songs of the season

Procession to the crib on Christmas Eve

O come, O come Emmanuel

St. Nicholas, pray for us

We prepare a place for you, O Lord.

What so ever you do to the least of my brothers, that you do unto me.

Come, Lord Jesus

What soever you do to the least of
my brothers, that you do unto me.

What soever you do to the least of
my brothers, that you do unto me

use these drawings for programs, invitations, cards or announcements

We wish you a merry Christmas

You have brought them abundant joy and great rejoicing

Merry Christmas

Community celebrations in Christmas week

I drink to you the love of St. John

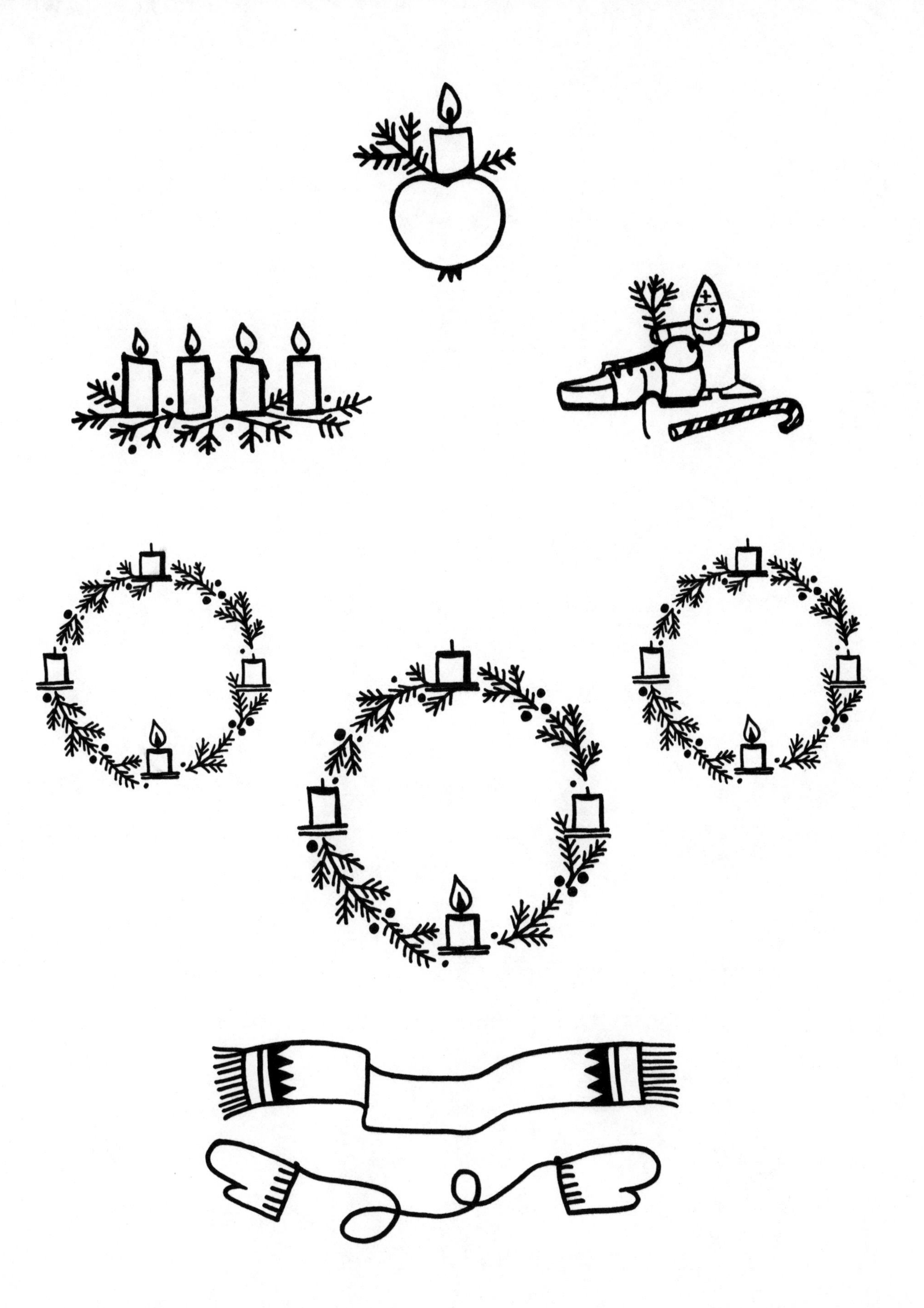

Advent
Christmas
Advent
Christmas
Blessed Christmas
Blessed Christmas
Shalom Peace
Shalom Peace
Your God is King
Your God is King
December 12

December 13

January

Epiphany

Lord, every nation on earth will adore you.

All Kings shall pay him homage,
all nations shall serve him

January 14

The motherhood of Mary

Upon you the Lord shines
and over you appears his
Glory!

They received a message in a
dream not to return to Herod

the Feast of the Epiphany

The Baptism of the Lord ·

He will baptize you in the Holy Spirit and in fire

This is my beloved Son, with him I am well pleased

[These illustrations also useful during the Advent Season]

One more powerful than I is to come after me

the star which they had observed at its rising went ahead of them

The Kings are brought to the stable

This is the Word of the Lord

Family and Community celebrations in the days of Epiphany.

Christ, bless this home

King, for a day!

the elected Kings!

Please come to our Party

January 19

January 20

February

Lenten themes

feast of the Presentation

A light to the revelation of the gentiles, and the glory of thy people Israel.

You shall do homage to the Lord your God; him alone shall you adore.

I will make you a great nation and I will bless you

He was transfigured before their eyes

Whoever drinks the water I give will never be thirsty

The Lord is my shepherd, there is nothing I shall want

So the man went off and washed and came back able to see

Father, I have sinned against God and against you

February 22

Lenten themes of the community in church

receiving ashes

Reconciliation

Praying the stations of the cross

Scripture study

February 23

Themes for St. Valentine's Day

Please come to a Valentine party

February 24

Make your own valentine using quotes or illustrations found on these pages

I shall take away their hearts
of stone
and give them
hearts of flesh

[From Ash Wednesday's liturgy but useful for a Valentine.]

You shall know they are
Christians by their Love

Where there is charity and
loving friendship
there is God

Themes for Mardi Gras or Shrove Tuesday
- for Valentine + Community Parties

As often as you did it for one
of my least brothers, you did
it for me.

As often as you did it for one
of my least brothers, you did
it for me.

As often as you did it for one
of my least brothers, you did
it for me.

February 28

The fasts of the rich
are the
feasts of the poor

Turn away from sin
and be faithful to
the Gospel

February 29

Prayer for the good of the soul
Fasting for the good of the body
Almsgiving for the good of our neighbor

prayer · fasting · almsgiving

prayer · fasting · almsgiving

The fasts of the rich
are the
feasts of the poor

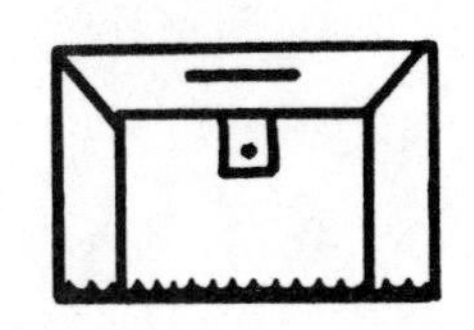

Turn away from sin
and be faithful to
the Gospel

March

Themes for Lent and Holy Week

Annunciation
March 25

Saint Patrick,
pray for us!

The Lord has put his faithful servant in charge of his household

St. Joseph

March 19

Hosannah! Blessed is He who comes in the name of the Lord

If there is love among you, all will know that you are my disciples

What I just did was to give you an example: as I have done, so you must do.

A new commandment I give you: Love one another as I have loved you

This is the wood of the cross, on which hung the Savior of the world. Come, let us worship.

We worship you, Lord,
we venerate your cross,
we praise your resurrection.
Through the cross you brought
joy to the world.

Upon him was the chastisement that makes us whole, by his stripes we were healed

Receive the Body of Christ

Love one another as I have loved you.

Good Friday

Bringing home palms

offeratory or almsgiving

The paschal meal

Celebrate the March wind

St. Patrick's day

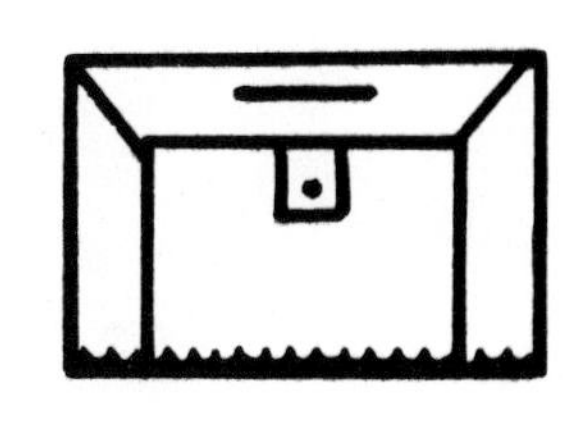

April

Easter themes

Alleluia · Alleluia · Alleluia

Alleluia · Alleluia · Alleluia

Come and eat your meal

Come and eat your meal

They knew him in the breaking of the bread

They knew him in the breaking of the bread

I saw water flowing
from the right side
of the temple, alleluia.
It brought God's life
and his salvation,
and the people sang in
joyful praise
Alleluia!

Doubt no longer, but believe

Themes from the Easter Vigil

Blessing of the fire and lighting of the candle

Rejoice, heavenly powers! Sing, choirs of angels!

By the power of the Spirit give to the water of this font the grace of your Son

Born again in Christ by baptism you have become members of Christ and of his priestly people

The readings

Themes for Easter springtime

A
Ω

ALLELUIA

A
Ω
A
Ω
ALLELUIA
ALLELUIA
A
Ω
ALLELUIA
April 44

May

Holy Mary pray for us

Joseph the worker

The Ascension

The visitation

Come Holy Spirit

Themes for May in the Parish Community

This is the word of the Lord

The Offertory

Processional for May devotion or the feast of Pentecost

Ascension Thursday

BINGO

Themes of May in the community

The school program

Happy Mother's Day

The Prom

June

Pentecost

Pentecost

Feast of the Trinity

Nativity of John the Baptist
June 24

Feast of Saints Peter and Paul June 29

Themes for June in Parish Community
Confirmation
Holy Matrimony
Themes for music and dance

Themes for June in family and community

Congratulations

School's out!

Happy Father's Day

June 56

July

Independence Day and Other Civic Observances

He spoke a message of peace and taught us to live as brothers. His message took form in the vision of our fathers as they fashioned a nation where people might live as one.

This message lives on in our midst as a task for us today and a promise for tomorrow.

Ward off the pride that comes
with worldly wealth and power
Give us the courage to open
ourselves in love to the service
of all your people

On high I dwell, and in holiness,
and with the crushed and
dejected in spirit, to revive the
spirits of the dejected, to revive
the hearts of the crushed.

Feast of Mary Magdalen July 22

Feast of Martha July 29

The Visitation of Mary and Elizabeth July 2

Lord are you not concerned that my sister left me alone to do the household tasks

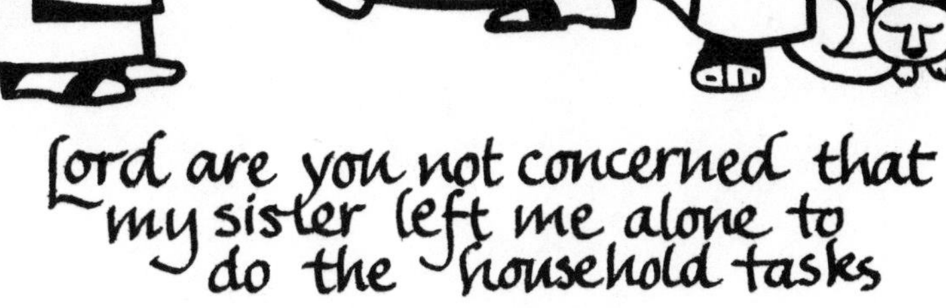

Lord are you not concerned that my sister left me alone to do the household tasks

Henceforth you will be catching men

Themes for
music or dance

Visit the sick

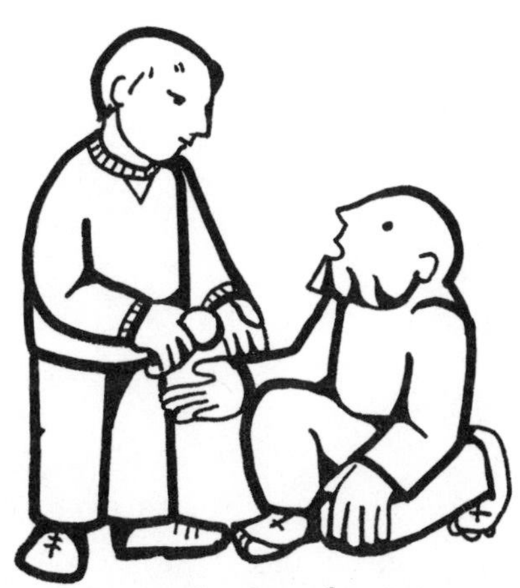

Feed the hungry

Ransom the captive

Bury the dead

Clothe the naked

Feed the hungry

Welcome the stranger

Give drink to the thirsty

themes for summer days, especially July

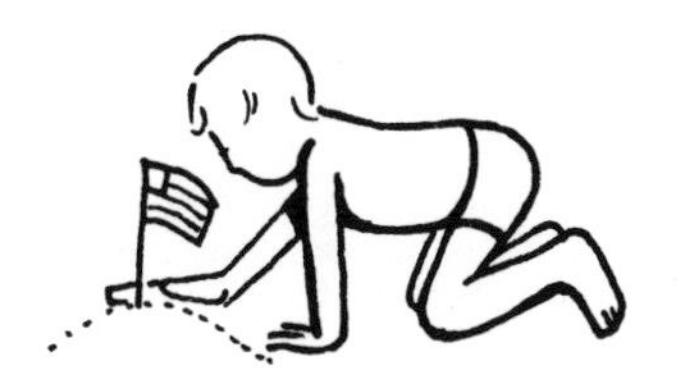

August

Blessed is
the womb
of the
Virgin Mary.
She carried
the Son of the
eternal Father

He was transfigured
before their eyes August 6

A great sign appeared
in heaven: a woman
clothed with the sun, the
moon beneath her feet,
and a crown of twelve
stars on her head

The Assumption · August 15

Themes for August in the Parish Community

Bless O Lord the Earth and her gifts to us

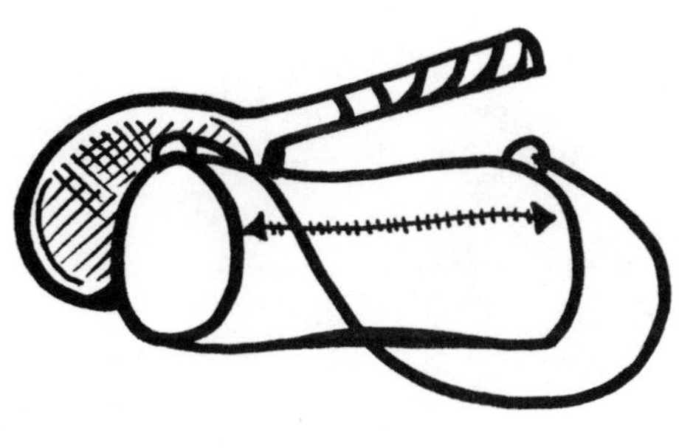

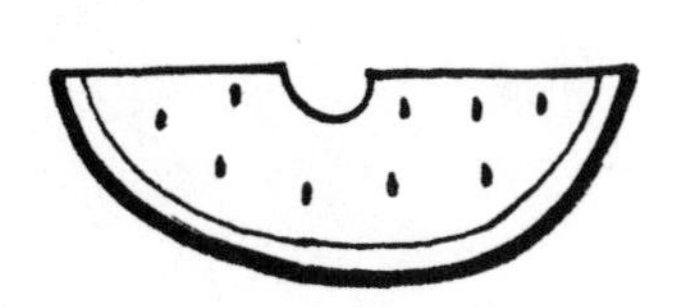

September

We adore you, O Christ, and we praise you because by your cross you have redeemed the world

Foxes have lairs and birds of the sky have nests

It is to just such as these that the Kingdom of God belongs

St. Michael, pray for us

Themes of work to celebrate Labor Day

Let the brightness of the Lord our God be upon us, and direct thou the works of our hands over us; the work of our hands do thou direct.

Themes for September in Community + family

October

St. Francis, pray for us

There is a lad here who
has five barley loaves
and a couple of dried fish

My angel will go before you.

See, I am sending an angel before you, to guard you on the way and bring you to the place I have prepared. Be attentive to him and heed his voice.

A blessing of pets
on the
Feast of St Francis

October 4

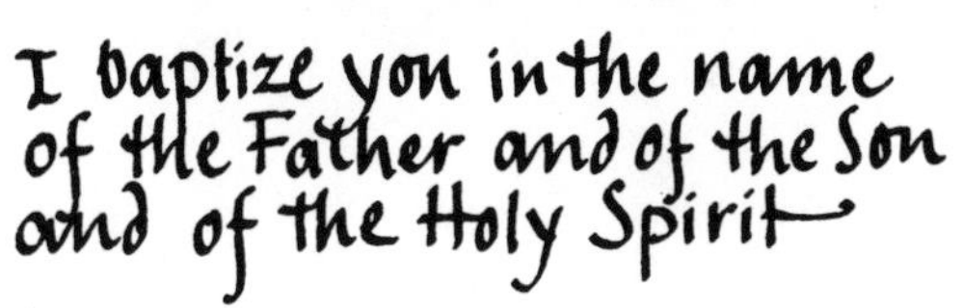

BAKE SALE

CAR WASH

Happy
Halloween

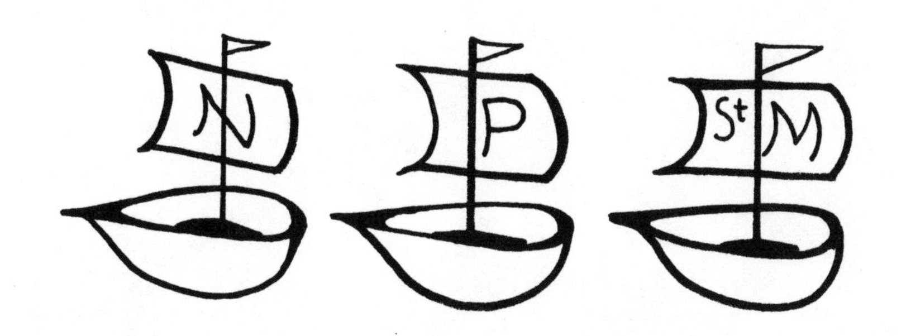
N
P
St M

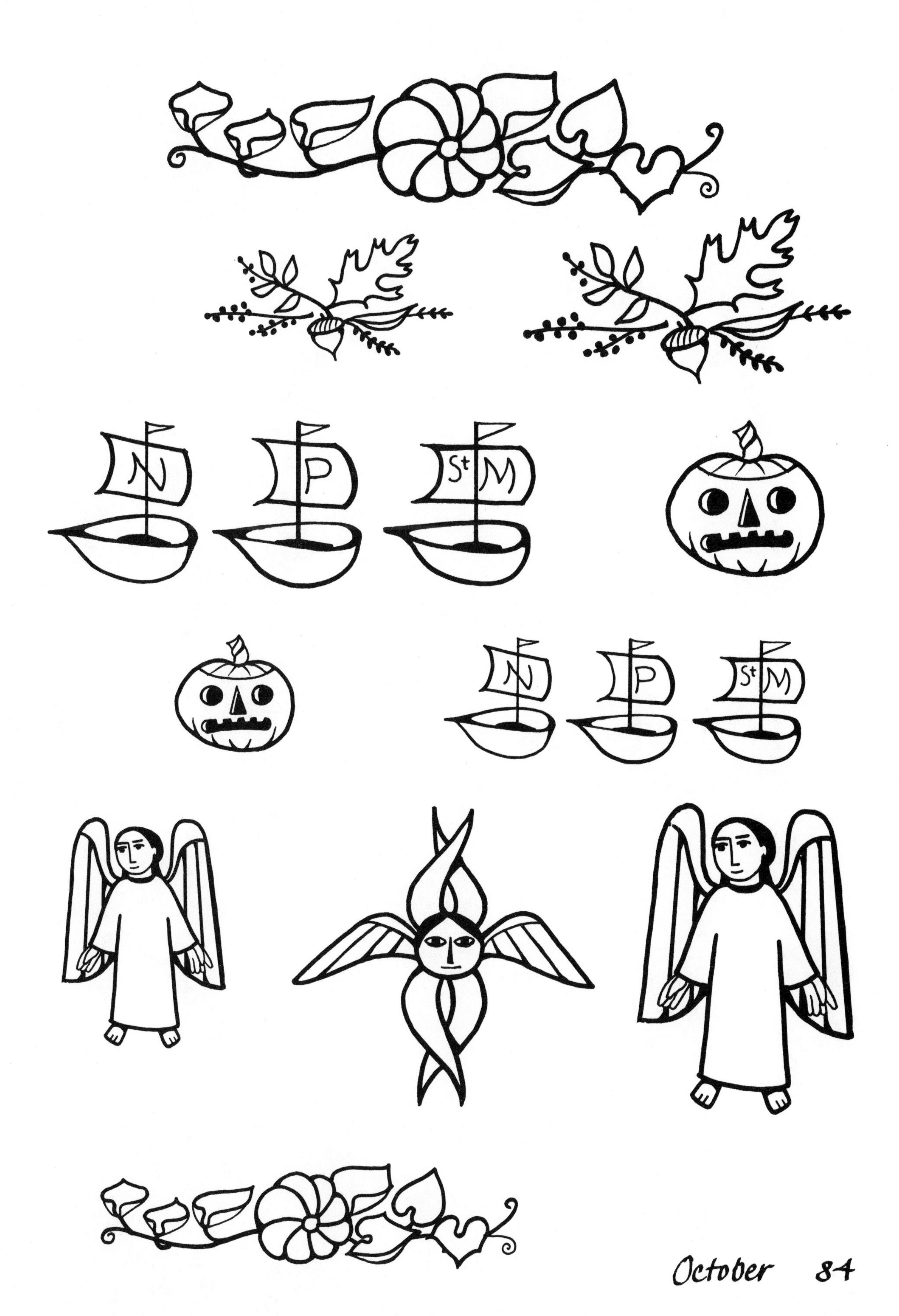
N
P
St M
N
P
St M

November

Lord, this is the people that longs to see your face.

Feast of Christ the King

God, who raised Jesus from the dead, will give new life to our own mortal bodies through his Spirit living in us.

Feast of All Souls

Bless the God of all who has done wondrous things on earth

We remember those who have gone before us

The earth has yielded its fruits God, our God has blessed us

November themes in school and home

Hearing or telling the stories of the saints

Themes for the lonely, the aged, the faithful departed

Give them eternal rest and may your light shine on them for ever

Let them share the joys and blessings of the life to come

I will give thanks to your name
because of your kindness and truth

VOTE ✓

VOTE ✓
VOTE ✓

Some Federal Holidays

Martin Luther King

Lincoln

George Washington

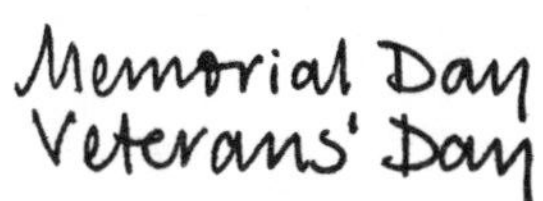

Columbus Day

Veterans' Day

Index

Index

Abraham, 21
Acorn, 83
Adoration of the Cross, 33, 34
Advent themes, 1, 6, 7, 8, 11, 16, 89
Advent wreath, 6, 7, 11, 89
Aged, 8, 24, 61, 62, 81, 88
Agony in the Garden, 32
All Saints Day, 85, 87
All Souls Day, 85, 86, 87
Alleluia, 38, 39, 43, 44
Almsgiving, 7, 8, 27, 28, 30, 35
Angel 1, 13, 31, 72, 79, 83
Angel, guardian, 79
Annunciation 1, 31
Apostles, 32, 59
Apple, 11, 12, 76, 77, picking, 82
Archangel Michael, 72
Artist, 74
Ascension, 45, 46
Ash Wednesday, 23, 30
Assumption, 66, 67
Assumption, blessing of herbs, 67, 70, 71
Autumn themes, 75--77, 81--84

Back-to-school, 75--77
Bake Sale, 81
Baker, 73
Baptism of adult, 41
Baptism of an infant, 80
Baptism of the Lord, 16
Baptism, themes of, 1, 16, 41, 45, 80
Baptismal water, 41
Baseball, 48, 58
Basketball, 48
Beach, 64, 65, 69
Bee, 64, 65
Bethlehem, 13, going to, 2, 3
Bible study, 23
Bingo, 47
Birdhouse, building, 74
Birds, 72, feeding, 81
Birthday, 64, 65, 68
Blessing of harvest, 67, 70, 71
76, 77, 82--84, 86, 89, 90, 91
Blessing of herbs, 67, 70, 71
Blessing of home, Epiphany, 18
Blessing of pets, 80
Blind man, 22
Boating, 63
Book, 76, 77
Bread and wine, 36, 37
Bug, 49, 50
Burial, 61, 86, 88
Businessman, 73, see also professions

Camping, 54
Candelabra, 36, 37
Canoeing, 63
Car Wash, 81
Cat, 18, 81
Cat and Mouse, 70, 71
Cattails, 76, 77
Charity, see almsgiving

Child with Guardian Angel, 79
Children, 1, 6, 7, 8, 9, 10, 17, 18,
19, 20, 21, 22, 26, 31, 34,
35, 41, 42, 46, 47, 48, 54,
60, 61, 63, 64, 65, 68, 69,
72, 73, 74, 75, 78, 79, 80,
81, 82, 86, 87, 88, 89
Choir 6, 8, 9, 53, 60
Christ and apostles, 59
Christ at the lakeside, 40
Christ Child, 2, 3, 4, 5, 15
Christ the King, 85
Christ with loaves and fishes, 78
Christ with Mary and Martha, 59
Christ with the children, 72
Christ with Thomas, 40
Christ, breaking bread, 40
Christ, teaching, 57
Christmas stocking, 7
Christmas themes 2--20.
Christmas tree, 13, 20
Christmas, family at, 9
Christmas wreath, 7
Civic observances, 57
Class room, 20, 75
Clean-up, 20
College, off to, 75
Columbus Day, 92
Columbus, ships of, 83, 84
Communion procession, 34
Computer, 74
Conductor, 74
Confession, Sacrament of, 23, 80
Confirmation, 53
Cookout, 69
Cross, 33, 72, 85, adoration of, 33, 34
Crucifixion, see cross

Dance, liturgical, 53
Death, see burial
Doctors, 74
Doves, 5

Easter basket, 42
Easter candle, 41, 43, 44
Easter eggs, 42, 43, 44
Easter fire, 41, 55
Easter foods, 43, 44
Easter lamb, 43, 44
Easter Sunday, going to church, 42
Easter themes, 38--44
Easter Vigil, 41
Easter water, blessing of font, 41
Elderly, see aged
Emmaus, 40
Epiphany, themes for, 14-20
Eucharist, symbol, 55, 56, 78
Exultet, 41

Family 7, 8, 9, 10. 18, 23, 34,
35, 42, 46, 48, 60, 61,
62, 68, 69, 75, 87, 88, 89
Family, Holy, 2, 3, 4, 5, 21

Farmer, 63, 73, 74, 81
Father, 7, 8, 9, 10, 18, 20, 23, 24
34, 35, 42, 46, 47, 60, 62,
68, 69, 73, 74, 75, 80,
81, 87, 88, 89, 92
Father's Day, 54
Feed the hungry, 7, 8, 27, 28,
30, 35, 61, 62; see also nee
Final Coming, 1
Fireworks, 63, 64, 65
First Communion, 34
Fish, 30, 31, 36, 37, 52, 55, 56
Flowers, 42, 43, 44, 47, 49, 50
64, 65, 70, 71, 90, 91
Fox has his lair, 72
Fruits, 55, 56, 67, 70, 71

Gabriel, 1
Ghosts, 82
Gift giving, 8, 9, 13, 24, 47, 58, 68
Good Friday, 33, 34
Good Shepherd, 22
Gospel reading, 17, 46
Graduation, 54, 55
Grandparents, 9, 47, 61, 74, 88
Grapes, 55
Guadalupe, Virgin of, 1, 66
Guardian angel, 79

Hairdresser, 73
Halloween, 82-84
Harvest, 67, 70, 71, 76, 77,
81, 82, 83, 84, 86,
89, 90, 91, 92
Harvesting, 81, 82
Herbs, 67, 70, 71, see blessing of
Hiking, 69
Holy Spirit, 16, 45, 51, 55
Holy Thurday, 32,
see also Agony in the Garden

Ice Cream, 55, 56
Ice skating, 10
Incense, 30, 31, 36, 37
Independence Day, 57, 63

Jack-o-lanterns, 82--84
Judgment, Christ in, 1
July 4th, see Independence Day

King, Martin Luther, 92
Kings, Three Holy, 14, 15, 17,
gifts of, 15
star of 15,
crowns of 15
dream, 15
Kiss of Peace, 60, 67
Kite flying, 35

Lamb, sacrificed, 36, 37
Pascal, 43, 44
Last Supper, 32
Leaves, 76, 77, raking, 81
Lector, 41, 67

Lenten themes, 21-37
Light house, 90, 91
Lincoln, Abraham, 92
Loaves and fishes, 55, 56, lad with 78
Lonely, 8, 9, 81, 88

Magi, see Kings
Mailbox, 90, 91
Martha and Mary, 59
Mary, see Virgin
Masquerade, 26
Matrimony, 53, 55, 56
Maundy Thursday, see Holy Thursday
May basket, 47
May day, 47
May devotion, 46
May Queen, 47
Meal, 10, 18, 19, 26, 27, 28, 35, 36, 37, 43, 44, 63, 64, 65, 78, 88, 89
Memorial day, 88, 92
Menorah, 36, 37
Mite box, 36, 37
Mittens, 11
Mother's Day, 48
Mother, 7, 8, 9, 10, 18, 19, 23, 24, 34, 35, 42, 46, 48, 60, 61, 62, 67, 68, 73, 75, 80, 87, 89
Music, 6, 8, 9, 53, 60, 64, 65, 68
Music, director, 60

Native American and Columbus, 92
Needy, 7, 8, 27, 28, 30, 35, 61, 62, 88

Offertory, 6, 35, 46, for the poor, 7, 8, 62
Offertory box, 29, 30, 36, 37

Palm, 36, 37
Palm Sunday, 31, 34, 35, 36, 37
Park bench, poor, 88
Party, dance, 26
  Epiphany, 18
  New Year, 10
  Seder, 35
  Shrove Tuesday, 26
  skating, 10
  skiing, 19
  tea, 10, 19
  winter, 19
  Valentine, 26
Passion, 33 see also cross
Peaceable Kingdom 1
Pencil, 76, 77
Penitent, 22, 80; see also reconciliation
Pentecost, 16, 51, 55
Pets, 18, 70, 71, 80, 81, blessing of, 80
Physical exam, 74
Piano, 68
Picnic, 63, 64, 65
Pieta, 33
Planting, 47, 49, 50, 63
Poor, see needy

Postman, 74
Presentation in Temple, 21
Presidents' Day, 92
Priest, 6, 17, 23, 34, 41, 46, 53, 60, 67, 80, 86
Private prayer, 60, 67
Procession, Ash Wednesday, 23
  Christmas Eve, 6
  Epiphany, 17, 18
  graduation, 54
  harvest, 67, 86
  into Jerusalem 31
  May, 46
  offertory, 6, 7, 8, 53
  Palm Sunday, 34
Prodigal son, 22
Prom, 48
Pumpkins, 82–84
Pupil, 8, 9, 20, 48, 54, 75

Rain, 42, 64, 65, 68
Ransom the captive, 61
Reader, 41, 67
Reading news, 87
Reconciliation, 22, 23, 60, 67, sacrament of, 23, 80
Refugees, 8, 27, 28, 58, 62
Risen Christ, 38, 39
Running, 68

School program, Christmas 9, music, 60, play, 48
School, back to, 75--77
School, end of, 54
Scripture study, 23
Secretary, 74
Seder supper, 35
Seeds, 47, 49, 50
Seniors, see aged
Sermon on the Mount, 57
Sheep, 13
Shepherds 4, 9
Shoes, buying new, 75
Shopping, 89
Sick, 8, 61
Singers, 48, 53, 54, 60, 68
Skating, 10
Skiing, 19
Snail, 70, 71
Snow, 9, 10, 19, 89
Snowmen, 19
Soccer, 68
Soup, 36, 37
Soup Kitchen, 27, 28, 36, 37, 88
Springtime themes, 42--44, 47, 49, 50
St. Francis, 78
St. John the Baptist, 1, 16, Nativity of, 52
St. Joseph, 2, 3, 4, 5, 31, 45, tools of, 36,
St Michael, 72
St. Nicholas 7, gifts from 11, 12
St. Patrick, 31, 35
Sts. Peter and Paul, 52

St. Thomas, 40
Star, 3, 12
Star gazing, 69
Stations of the Cross, praying the 23
Story telling, 59, 61, 72, 87, 88
Straws for manger 7
Suffering, see Agony in the Garden,
  see blind man,
  see lonely,
  see needy,
  see Passion,
  see pieta,
Summer themes, 47–50, 63–71
Sun and Moon, 70, 71
Surgeon, 74

Teacher, 9, 20, 61, 75–77
Telephoning, 87
Temple, Child Jesus in, 5, 21
Temptation in desert, 21
Tennis, 63, 70, 71
Thanksgiving, 83, 84, 86, 89, 90, 92
Tools of St. Joseph, 36, 37
Tools, garden, 49, 50, 76, 77
Transfiguration, 21, 66
Triduum, see Holy Thursday, Good Friday, Easter Vigil
Trinity, 52

Vacation, family, 69
Valentine themes, 24-26
Vegetables, 67, 70, 71, 83, 86
Veterans Day, 90, 92
Virgin, 1
  Annunciation, 1, 31
  Assumption, 66
  devotion to, 46
  enthroned 45, 66
  Guadalupe, 66
  Visitation, 45, 59
Visit the prisoner, 61
Visit the sick, 8, 61
Visitation, 45, 59
Visiting the aged/lonely, 61, 88
Voting day, 90, 91

Walking in the woods, 82, 89
Washing of feet, Peter, 32, parishoner, 34
Washington, George, 92
Watermelon, 70, 71
Wedding, 53, 55, 56
Welcome the stranger, 62
Wheat, 55, 56
Whitsunday, 51, 55
Winter themes, 2--30, 89-91
Wise men, see Kings
Witches, 82
Woman at the well, 22
Women at the tomb, 38, 39
Women, feasts of, 67
Wood pile, 90, 91
Worker, 73, 74